I0011204

Adapting to the New World of I.T.
Mini-Book Strategy Series – Book 5

Author: Rand Morimoto, Ph.D.

ISBN: 1542689996
ISBN-13: 978-1542689991

DEDICATION

I dedicate this book to my youngest son Eduardo, who helped me select the photos for this book, and inspires me to always work hard and to keep current on the latest technologies and business solutions.

TABLE OF CONTENTS

INTRODUCTION

The adoption of cloud technologies, like hosted email, file sharing, Web conferencing, and public cloud hosted servers is no longer a short-term fad, but the new norm for enterprises and their employees. Mainstream cloud services have proven to be reliable, secure, and cost effective for organizations leading to the proliferation of cloud services across ALL systems and applications throughout enterprises.

However, with the proliferation of cloud technologies in organizations comes a need for change in how information technology (I.T.) departments manage technologies and technical services, and a change in how users interact and "consume" cloud services. For organizations just completing their migration to cloud services, I.T.'s role and user's interaction with cloud services tend to remain the same for a while.

Once the dust settles though, I.T. departments realize that they no longer have physical servers to build, maintain, monitor, and manage. A reassessment of the "footprint" of datacenters and the associated equipment in those datacenters results in active decommissioning and "rightsizing" of I.T. systems and operations. For end users that for years experienced a disruptive major upgrade every 4-7 years of their computer systems and applications will find new features, new versions of applications automatically updated every month or even every week.

The rolling update and upgrade process provides users with a great benefit of not having to wait years before a new feature is added, nor does it require users to scramble around to find some 3rd party plug-in to add in to their applications to help them with some integrated task. In the cloud app world, most of the time users just have to wait a few weeks and a sorely needed feature is slipped in during a rolling update.

These dynamic changes to user applications and experiences should not be suppressed by organizations but rather openly embraced as part of the new norm, paving the path for a better way of supporting the new world of I.T. It is these changes in policies and processes based on best practices from real world experiences that is highlighted throughout the pages of this book.

Part I:
Cloud Computing as a Business Model

1 THE REALIZATION THAT CLOUD COMPUTING IS HERE TO STAY

It has been a good 7-8 years since early versions of cloud solutions like Google Docs, Box.com, DropBox, and Salesforce started to appear in the marketplace, with early adopters grasping hold of these new technologies to fulfill a particular need they had. But it has really been in the past 3-4 years that significant migrations by mainstream Corporate America enterprises to standardize on cloud services that legitimized cloud computing as being here to stay.

Made for the Cloud, not just Branded as the Cloud

The difference that a half-decade made from early early adopters to mainstream enterprises in the adoption of the cloud was supported by key cloud vendors actually redeveloping their applications to be optimized for cloud specific operations. Early cloud solutions by many providers were simply the same old product they've been selling for years stuffed into a hosted datacenter. The early solutions did not scale well, and early cloud solutions also had problems with uptime and reliability as the cloud providers were figuring out how to truly provide a 24x7x365 offering with millions of users around the globe.

In the past couple years though, now 2 or 3 generations of software built specifically for the cloud later, and datacenter operational practices built to truly provide non-stop global operations, cloud has provided a reliable and stable platform that organizations expect from their application service providers.

Cloud-based File Sharing as the Early Entrant to the Enterprise

Collaborative File Sharing was one of the first cloud hosted services to enter mainstream enterprises. File sharing services like DropBox, Box.com, and Google Docs filled a need users weren't getting from their inhouse I.T. departments of being able to access files and to share files with anyone, from any device, from anywhere, at any time. Most enterprise filesystems a decade ago were internal Microsoft Windows-based network shares that were only accessible from inside the corporate network (or through a limited-access VPN remote connection) that did not facilitate sharing of the files with non-employees. And as Apple iPhones, iPads, and Android mobile devices sprang up a decade ago, users wanted to be able to access and share files from their non-Windows based devices as well.

Services from these file and collaboration providers allowed easy access and sharing of content all during the 2008-2010 timeframe in the midst of a global recession when organizations had other things it was worrying about. During this "perfect storm" of new devices, need for access, lack of enforcement by enterprises, and the rise of cloud-based file sharing solutions did early cloud services arise. By the time I.T. departments realized they had a major hole in their security with users openly sharing sensitive data outside of the Corporate firewall, it was too late to rein in cloud-based file sharing, so the path most enterprises have taken over the past couple years has simply been to wrap security and controls around the external shares and adopt cloud file sharing as the new norm for the organization.

Cloud-based Electronic Mail as the Enterprise Standard

While cloud-based file sharing slipped its way in to enterprises through the backdoor, it was cloud-based Electronic Mail (email) systems that were the first I.T. sanctioned foray into the cloud. Today, most enterprises have migrated their email systems to a cloud service like Microsoft's Office 365 or Google's G Suite, or at least have plans to migrate their email systems to the cloud in upcoming cycles.

Email systems were ripe for outsourcing because of the high visibility email had as a critical business application, but the difficulty in truly making email highly reliable and geographically redundant. While Microsoft's Exchange Server system provided a very effective geo-database replication technology in its offering, to do it right, organizations had to have two or more geographically distributed sites, with high speed network connectivity, high powered servers, and a lot of expensive disk storage to make it all work properly. It's a VERY costly solution for 90% of the enterprises out there to implement and support a solution of this type, whereas a cloud hoster that provides email as a service to millions of users can make this level of email redundancy and reliability cost effective.

Add to this cloud offering migration tools that made the migration to cloud-based hosted email "easy," no different that migrating from an older version of an on-premise email system to the latest release of the on-premise email system, but instead to the cloud, organizations adopted cloud-based email systems in mass.

Cloud-based Application Integration Takes Hold

With enterprises typically running Microsoft's Office 365 for their cloud-hosted email, plus a hodge-podge list of cloud-based file sharing solutions, once organizations were comfortable with their Exchange email in the cloud, the task of integrating email with their file sharing services was the logical first step in cloud-based application integration. Because organizations already owned Microsoft's OneDrive file sharing solution, along with significant upgrades and improvements Microsoft made to their file sharing technology to support non-Microsoft endpoints as well as better collaborative capabilities, migration of content from Box.com, Google Docs, and other file sharing solutions to OneDrive started to take place.

For other cloud-based solutions like Salesforce.com for enterprise relationship management services, or Workday for employee resource management, the integration of these cloud applications into an organization's cloud-based email and file sharing set in motion the cloud-to-cloud integration of services. This cloud app integration has been a major focus for I.T. departments as they look to improve access between applications used by employees throughout their enterprise.

Depending on Cloud Reliability

While early cloud solutions were prone to outages and downtime, with a few years of operational best practices in place and behind them, the mainstream cloud providers can now provide highly reliable online services to their customers. Additionally, as subscriptions to cloud services now number in the millions of seats for these large providers, the investment in geo-redundancy and real time replication and management is more easily absorbed into the cost of operations.

For enterprises to implement the same redundant datacenter services spread out across hundreds or even a few thousand users, cloud hosted providers spread that same cost across millions of users. Cloud scale simply makes it cheaper for large hosters to provide better services at a significantly lower cost than any enterprise can do on their own. And it is this investment that mainstream cloud providers have put into their operations to ensure their customers receive the level of high performance and reliability they expect.

Relying on Cloud Security

Along with high performance and reliability comes security. With cyber-attacks on the rise, the security and protection of enterprise data is crucial for organizations. The same investment cloud hosted providers get to spread out across millions of users for replication and reliability technologies, the cloud hosted providers do the same for security and data protection systems. The mainstream cloud providers know their reputations are based on their ability to protect the security and integrity of their client's data, and their investments are spread out across millions and tens of millions of users. No enterprise can invest the same amount in security at the same cost per user than the large-scale cloud providers.

Additionally, because cloud hosted providers have thousands of customer organizations, and billions of email messages and files under management, the sheer volume of data makes it harder for a hacker to target data compared to attacking a single enterprise like Sony, Home Depot, or Target stores.

Realizing Cost Effectiveness

The economies of scale drives costs down for the largest cloud providers, spreading out the investments in security and reliability across tens of millions of users, making it effectively impossible for enterprises to implement the same level of services at a lower cost. As cloud providers look to attract even more customers, many of the barriers that once gave enterprises a pause in subscribing to a cloud subscription have been removed. A shift from locked in 3-year contracts to now month-by-month pricing, and a shift from all-or-nothing bundles to a la carte pricing models provides organizations options that meet their needs.

For enterprises that completed their migrations a year or two ago, they are finally getting around to "letting go" of their old on-premise systems and decommissioning old servers, purging old archives, and freeing up datacenter space to finally realize the cost savings of being solely in the cloud for their applications. By releasing racks and racks of servers and systems, organizations are finding their datacenter footprints are now in many cases cut in half, allowing for an overall cost savings on I.T. expenditures.

Simpler I.T. infrastructures have resulted in simpler I.T. management systems, lower ongoing capital expenditures, and a minimization of related costs of services that the true cost savings of cloud computing are finally being realized by enterprises.

2 UNDERSTANDING THE NEW OPPORTUNITIES BROUGHT ON BY CLOUD COMPUTING

The shift away from the on-premise models to cloud services has brought about awareness of I.T.'s new role with a focus on the business and not on blinking lights in the datacenter. Organizations are now able to invest in business focused solutions not on building and managing a global network of expensive datacenters and security systems.

Focusing on Business Solutions

With less of a focus on servers and systems, I.T. departments and businesses as a whole have been able to explore and invest in solutions that benefit the frontline of their organizations. I.T. departments have been able to repurpose key personnel that used to spend their time architecting vast capital intensive overhead costing datacenter environments to instead focus their time helping increase revenues and decrease costs in all parts of the organization through the use of technological systems.

I.T. departments are spending their time and effort on finding ways to help their organizations increase frontline sales, decrease manufacturing and shipping times, improve internal and external communications, and better manage operational processes. I.T. services are now focused on improving the bottomline of their businesses, than simply keeping email systems, file sharing systems, and buildings of server equipment operational.

Focusing on People

With a focus on frontline operations of their businesses, I.T. is also getting outside of the confines of the datacenters and getting out to interact with the employees of the organization. The more I.T. understands what employees do and what the frontline of their organization does, the more the I.T. solution architects can identify ways that technology can better support and assist personnel in their organization to do things "better."

It is this shift from architecting and designing fancy "computer systems" to architecting and designing business solutions is the shift that I.T. organizations go through in the value they bring to their organizations.

Sorting Needs to the Importance in Business Success

Just like with any list of needs, the key is to sort the needs and prioritize them so that I.T. can focus on the most important business solutions first. Of course the huge concern for I.T. organizations right now is the fact that there are a lot of these external cloud-based services where sensitive business documents are stored, without any security oversight, so the organization wants to move quickly to lock down content and protect information as quickly as possible. However rather than blocking access and preventing access to external information, the organization can sort business user needs into importance around business success, and then I.T. can get its arms around the technology solution needs in proper order.

Sorting Needs to the Fundamentals of Business Operations

The fundamentals of business operation are typically to help the organization meet its business goals. In many organizations, it's the things that help increase revenues that contribute directly to business profitability. When properly implemented and supported, those tools can help contribute to the success of the organization. From a technology standpoint, it might be tools that help sales individuals better target customer needs, which might be a client relationship management tool, or data analysis tools that crunches and processes data. Or it could be public awareness tools that help individuals within an organization better communicate with the organization's customers, that are of most benefit to the organization.

For many organizations, e-mail is a fundamental business tool, as users may use email to communicate with customers. Others may find transaction processing tools like ERP tools as mission critical for the business in terms of accepting and processing orders for shipment. Every organization has fundamental business needs that are supported by technology, and those tools that have the most impact on the success of the business are the ones that are typically prioritized for fulfillment in I.T.'s strategy implementation roadmap.

Reconciling Needs and Establishing I.T. Priorities

Reconciling needs may sound very similar to sorting fundamental business needs and priorities, but the focus here is I.T. priorities. There may be conflicting priorities that need to be addressed, and those may need to be rolled up to management to prioritize what is deemed most important to the organization. One example is an outward facing client solution that may drive sales up, however at the same time a security concern like customer and confidential legal information stored in unprotected external cloud storage services may need to be addressed promptly as well. Effectively one priority can improve business revenues, whereas another priority addresses data leakage due to lack of security controls.

In cases where there are conflicting business priorities, a business decision needs to be made to determine what the organization will prioritize. Many times, leveraging contract resources can allow an organization to do two or more things at the same time. Alternatively, the organization can do a risk assessment and while protecting confidential information is extremely important, if the data has been hosted externally at a cloud provider for the past 2 years, then what's another few more weeks to get around to tightening down the security on the external content. There are pros and cons, and establishing I.T. priorities can address the timing and fulfillment of execution on I.T. initiatives within the enterprise.

I.T.'s Success is Measured on Business Success

What we've seen over the past couple years is a shift in the measurement of whether I.T. is successful or not. In the past, I.T. measured its success typically by its attainment of some measurement of service level reliability of I.T. systems. If the organization's goal is 99.99% uptime, then the organization drives to that measurement and says it is successful because systems were always operational.

However, the more recent measurements of I.T. success have been based on the success of the business. When I.T. can associate increases in profitability with the introduction of a key sales tool or data analysis tool that helped the organization be more effective selling, then I.T. can show measurable contribution to the financial success of the organization. Or I.T. can directly translate the lowering of costs in the organization, like the decrease in long distance phone call bills, or the reduction in travel costs through the introduction of Web Conferencing or Web-based telephony solutions. The Web-based solution can better support users to communicate over existing data connections rather than using phone line services that charge per minute.

When the organization has the opportunity to grow and expand and to do so without direct linear increases in costs, this becomes a win for the I.T. department, if its services were key to that measurement of success within the business.

Focusing on Business Results, not Operational Capacity

Lastly, another metric for measurement is the shift from measuring I.T.'s value in terms of meeting operational capacity - shifting to measuring I.T.'s ability to directly address business results. If employees of an organization can communicate effectively with their clients using fewer travel days having to go and meet clients in person: not only are there direct savings in travel costs, but the employee can be spending the time normally consumed by travel to be communicating with other clients and helping expand the business.

The shift to cloud-based services with elastic capacity eliminates the need for the I.T. department to track and manage operational capacity. Instead, I.T. can now focus its time and effort on adding additional services, providing better methods of communications, and directly focusing the efforts of the business to grow and expand its services to the community.

3 COMPLETING THE JOURNEY TO THE CLOUD

For enterprises that have already migrated their email to a cloud hosted provider and potentially integrated cloud-based file sharing and collaboration as part of its business services, it is that "next step" in an organization's journey that'll help the organization complete their path to application and datacenter modernization.

The Hybrid Strategy – Not Just Migrating to the Cloud

As much as the first couple chapters of this book have focused on talking about hosted cloud applications or cloud computing, in reality, the cloud is just ONE option for the target destination of application modernization. The goal for organizations is application and datacenter modernization, not necessarily just cloud migration. A hybrid strategy that includes some applications that remain on-premise, and some applications that are migrated to the cloud have been found to be the norm for organizations modernization their I.T. operations.

Cloud as an Option, Not the Total End Goal

The end goal for any I.T. organization is to truly optimize their I.T. operations. In basic economic terms, I.T. should leverage the most efficient and effective services that fulfill on the business requirements of the organization at an optimized cost. Early cloud solutions did not meet the security or reliability requirements of many organizations, and thus 2 or 3 years ago, the cloud wasn't the best solution for many of these organizations. However, over time, the cloud providers have improved and optimized their services, and are now providing mature, highly secure, and reliable services that organizations have to seriously consider as part of their application modernization initiatives.

Many organizations have tried to bundle up their existing highly customized applications, forklift them into the cloud, and then run them in a cloud hosted environment only to find that the cost of running the application isn't cheaper and in many cases significantly more expensive to run a specific application outside of the internal datacenter. In those cases, cloud was not the best choice for a cost or performance perspective. There are several factors in assessing the true efficiencies of the application and datacenter modernization plan that are highlighted throughout the text of this book.

Focusing on App and Datacenter Modernization

While the title of this chapter is "Completing the Journey to the Cloud," it's not about taking 100% of everything being run on-premise today and moving of it to the cloud. The focus on modernization is to clearly assess the use of the application, preferably working from the perspective of the users themselves to determine WHAT the users can most effectively use in their day to day responsibilities.

In early engagements in application and datacenter modernization efforts, in some cases it was found that many employees don't find the applications they are using particularly helpful in completing the tasks of their jobs. Whether that application is on-premise or in the cloud, an ineffective application is an ineffective application for these users. When the day to day tasks of a user is assessed and analyzed, a completely different application is found to be more applicable for those users.

In some cases, the idea of "modernization" has been to completely replace an existing on-premise application with a completely new and different application. In other cases, a Software as a Service (SaaS) application exists that the users are able to take advantage of that is immediately available and provides significant value to the users. Key SaaS

16

examples include accounting applications, client relationship management applications, and human resource management applications.

Many organizations have been using the same accounting software for years, repeatedly upgrading the software every 5-10 years, but finding the function of the general ledger, accounts payable application, and accounts receivable application being sufficient for the organization. However key integration components like time and billing systems, expense report systems, client management systems, project costing, and cost accounting systems integrated into the application are frequently found to be grossly inadequate. The modern SaaS applications have evolved to provide extensive features and functions that enable employees using tablets or mobile phones to quickly enter their timesheets or file expense reports without having to sit in front of a "computer" and a legacy "web browser", instead getting key components of their work done from a readily available mobile app.

It's this type of thinking, assessment, analysis, and business optimization that truly modernizes how organizations improve their business bottom-line. It's that shift from a legacy on-premise application to do the same thing in the cloud that might be more up to date, more functional, and easier to support that is advancing the organization into a modern application environment.

The On-Premise Model for Legacy Applications

One key example of applications remaining on-premise rather than being simply migrated to the cloud are very old customized legacy applications. Some organizations have spent months updating the code or rewriting their legacy applications to support a cloud-model without a lot of thought into understanding how the application is used, and whether the application in its legacy form (now migrated to the cloud) actually serves the organization.

Instead, the application should be assessed, users of the application interviewed to determine "who" uses the application, "what" they use the application for, and "whether" the application actually serves a valuable function to the organization. Or could the same function and utility be achieved with a different application altogether?

With all the applications a typical organization has, it is these old legacy applications that are frequently best off being assessed and dealt with last. The organization can gain more traction and better time utilization by focusing on other applications that may be more effectively migrated to the cloud or modernized, and circle back to these legacy applications later.

These legacy applications may be good candidates to just continue to have them run on-premise, and thus a clear justification of a hybrid model where applications are migrated to the cloud, modernized to a new model, or just left on-premise as the near-term strategy of the organization.

Potentially Migrating Core Secure Apps Last

Another key set of applications that are best to leave on-premise are applications that have extremely high security or regulatory compliance requirements wrapped around the application. Rather than spending months trying to create the ultimate secure cloud environment, an organization can better allocate their time and efforts identifying and migrating "all the other applications" in the enterprise that are easier or cleaner to modernize and migrate, and leave the more complex or compliance-restricted applications on-premise to be the last to deal with in modernizing and migrating.

This strategy has proven successful for enterprises as they move email, file collaboration, backup systems, intranet content, accounting software, and the like to cloud-based systems, gain experience with the cloud providers for their reliability and security features, and then make more informed and easier decisions down the line on core specialized applications.

The Larger the Enterprise, the More Likely the Hybrid Model for I.T.

Small organizations with fewer than 300 employees have been successful in modernizing almost "all" of their application and datacenter services into the cloud within a few months with the initial migration of core business productivity applications to Office 365. Subsequent migrations have included initiatives to move the accounting and line of business applications to a SaaS or IaaS VM-based cloud model, and finally leveraging hosted endpoint and server management tools thereafter. But the larger the enterprise, the longer it will take to modernize and optimize applications and the datacenter. It's clear that the modernization process could take months or even years to complete and, as such, a hybrid model is the norm for these larger enterprises.

A huge challenge for large enterprises is simply getting around to all of the application owners across hundreds of applications to do the business analysis assessment of who uses the application, what the application is used for, and whether there is a better way of handling the application with an off the shelf SaaS application, a refactor to a PaaS application, the simple migration of the application to an IaaS virtual machine in the cloud, or whether the application should just remain on-premise.

18

However, despite the fact that larger enterprises are more complicated and will take longer to modernize their applications and datacenters, this doesn't mean that the large enterprises cannot benefit from the cloud economies of scale. Quite the contrary, the larger the enterprise, the more inefficiencies exist in terms of duplication of similar application function and services, or simply just the operations, support, and management of "systems" that are either under-utilized or even not used at all. In one environment assessment, it was found that of the 480 applications identified by the organization, 120 of the applications were running on servers, backed up daily, and configured for replication and high availability, yet NO users actually used the applications any longer.

So an analysis and assessment for organizations of all sizes net out a significant benefit simply by optimizing I.T. operations and business services to meet the current needs of the organization.

Planned and Coordinated Transitions to Modernization

Application and datacenter modernization efforts are likened to the work done almost a couple decades ago in Y2K assessments, where every application in the organization is identified, key application owners are identified, and the purpose and use of the application documented. In a very methodical process, an organization can quickly identify how application and datacenter modernization can be conducted in the organization, with categorization of applications that will be the easiest to modernize, versus applications that fit in the category of not appropriate to modernize (or be prioritized last), and everything in-between.

This planned and coordinated transition process can take an organization months or even years to complete, with some logical milestones that include modernizing an application during a typical migration or upgrade cycle. So if an application is upgraded every 4-years and the 4th year comes along, rather than just upgrading the application to the next on-premise version, instead take that opportunity to assess and modernize the application.

Without additional cost, effort, or commitment to time historically allocated for application upgrades and updates, the organization can more rapidly transition to newer, more appropriate and effective applications.

Getting to the Rest of I.T.

Usually in the application and datacenter modernization process, organizations start with transition efforts around migrating email to the cloud, or implementing dev and test scenarios in a cloud-based solution, or replacing legacy applications with specialized SaaS based services. The "rest of I.T." in the transition process takes a holistic approach to all applications and services run by the organization.

The other services may include user identity and authentication, it usually includes backup and business continuity solutions, and it includes management systems. The reason these other services are specifically called out is that, as organizations shift from a datacenter model to a distributed cloud-based model, monitoring systems isn't as simple as loading an agent on all of the servers in a datacenter and monitoring the systems. In the new cloud based model, it may require doing application state monitoring across a number of different cloud-based IaaS, PaaS, and SaaS environments and in some hybrid cases an on-premise environment.

Patch and update management systems in an environment based on cloud services may no longer be needed, as SaaS-based applications typically have no tenant level patching and updating responsibilities. Even for the handful of systems that are left in the datacenter, or the handful of systems that are running as IaaS virtual machines in a cloud environment, the organization has to think whether an enterprise scale server management tool is needed anymore. It was fine having an enterprise grade management system when the organization had 50, 500, 5000 systems to manage, but when the organization is left with a fraction of the number of systems, a simpler solution for management might be to use a basic Windows Update platform, or even a manual process that takes someone in I.T. a couple hours a month to initiate and manage may be more efficient than having a team of people monitoring and managing the management system each day and week.

So the process of modernizing "everything else" in the datacenter may very likely be selectively choosing systems to eliminate and not need any plans for replacement.

Transitioning the Rest of the Datacenter Isn't a One for One Process

Another interesting lesson learned in transitions out of a traditional datacenter model to a modern cloud model is the benefit that consolidation plays in the transition process. Rather than taking 100 servers and migrating the servers to 100 cloud-based servers, the I.T. organization needs to assess a model where consolidation can reduce the footprint of the enterprise.

While the organization may have 100 servers, through consolidation of services such as adding multiple database instances to a single database server, or consolidating multiple web instances to a single (or handful) of servers can decrease the sheer number of systems that'll reside in the I.T.

environment down the line.

Many times application servers were built to host a specific application without consideration that the application could co-run on an existing system. During the initial implementation process, application owners are typically target focused on the deployment of their application, not on datacenter optimization. So a simple process of stepping back, identifying applications, and then consolidating applications to fewer systems will help maximize the efficiency of I.T. in the organization, and best optimize the environment as part of the modernization process.

Other applications were built to run in distributed datacenters to be "closer to users," however in this day and age of high speed wide area network connectivity and latency insensitive communication protocols, applications can be centralized without the need to put a server in each and every site. As an example, a content sharing system may have been implemented in 6 site datacenters of the organization, distributing the application infrastructure and enabling close access to localized data for each organizational site. However, in a modernization effort where the application is consolidated to a cloud-based environment, potentially just 1 or 2 distributed cloud-based instances of the application is now needed, thus eliminating the need for a lot of redundant infrastructure. Just as the organization in years prior were assessed on performance and redundancy, a new assessment can be conducted to determine if the high-speed connectivity options available today will be sufficient to consolidate the application across a single region instead of six.

These are all of the tasks that need to be considered as part of the completion of datacenter modernization. Not simply taking each application and moving them one-to-one into a similarly configured hosted environment, but instead conducting a thorough into a more appropriate modern model that still meets the core needs of the organization.

Part II:
Cloud Computing's Impact on End User Interaction

4 SUPPORTING THE KNOWLEDGEABLE WORKFORCE

One of the factors in the shift to the new world of I.T. that goes beyond the evolution of technologies and the proliferation of cloud services focuses simply on a better digitally skilled workforce. All things tech related are no longer solely a realm for techies. Two decades ago, the average office worker had limited computer experience and had to be trained to use a piece of software, and systems were built and configured to simplify the learning experience. However with a tech savvy workforce with new entrants to the workforce that know nothing but a world filled with computers, search engines, and the Internet along with a senior workforce that has been using systems daily for the past decade or more, knowledge and experience of technology is no longer just in the datacenter.

The Knowledgeable Workforce

Those entering the workforce today are a whole generation of individuals who were born and raised at a time when the Internet was pervasive throughout their lives. These individuals know how to work an online search engine better than they would know what to do in a library with a card catalog. They've had no fewer than two mobile devices they've setup and configured on their own, and downloading and figuring out "apps" is old hat for them.

And not just the entering workforce, but also the Gen-Y's and Gen-X'ers that have also spent more of their time on computers and the Internet than with typewriters, books, pen and paper, are just as tech savvy. With a more tech savvy workforce, the idea that the datacenter and anything "systems related" is exclusive to the I.T. staff has drastically changed as tech knowledge and expertise has clearly distributed to the masses.

The current workforce, young and old, is not afraid of new tech tools, new digital ways of doing things, and in fact they embrace the integration of technology into their day-to-day work efforts as they typically have better tools and better technology now at home or in their pockets than they're provided at the office.

Social media is a communications medium that a good portion of this new workforce has personally used in their distribution of information to a personal network of distributed users. The reading of printed newsletters, newspapers, and lengthy emails has given way to a world of short SMS text messages, 160-character Twitter feeds, shared photos with 1 line captions, and simple likes, dislikes, and emoticons.

Empowering Not Impeding Productivity

With a more tech savvy workforce, I.T. needs to empower the workforce with tools and resources that help the workers be more effective in their jobs. I.T. needs to stop "locking down systems" intended to prevent workers from accidentally breaking their systems, to making systems and processes more open to new and innovative ways of getting the job done.

The workforce installs apps, configures apps, replaces their devices and reinstalls their apps on a regular basis on their own personal phones and tablets, so they don't necessarily need a fully configured system with the exact same icons in the exact same spot to figure out how to use their systems at the office. Granted, there are many organizations where there are a handful of users that require handholding, and many times those that need the most handholding are the most vocal. However understand the entire workforce, and if 10% of the workforce needs help, no need to build monolithic processes across the entire environment to support a smaller and smaller portion of those needing extra assistance.

Organizations that are able to empower their workforce to do more and to push the limits of the technology in front of them are providing their workforce with the ability to be more effective at what they do. We've called it "worker productivity" in years past and used to relate it to the increase in productivity of using a word processor to write and edit documents rather than a typewriter, or the use of email to send communications to many people than writing memos, photocopying the memos, and manually distributing the memos to users. But in this day and age, worker productivity can be enhanced by allowing the worker to use digital tools and communications mechanisms that help them be more effective at getting messages across, sharing information, and collaborating with co-workers.

I.T. departments know darn well if they don't give their workers tools they can use, the users will just sign-up for a cloud-based service on their own and use tools outside of the organization to do what they feel is best for getting their job done. So I.T. either embraces the tools and technologies the current workforce wants to leverage, or I.T. spends its time trying to prevent users from using tools and blocking productivity.

Focusing Less on the Device, and More on the Applications

Another drastic change in the I.T. industry is the movement away from managing the device, and more focus on providing applications to users. For the past decade, I.T. has provided users a device typically with Microsoft Windows loaded on it pre-configured with all of the applications the user needed. The device was locked down and tightly managed.

However as the typical user has 3 or 4 devices these days (mobile phone, tablet, laptop, office computer) of which many of these devices are not even owned and managed by the organization, does focusing on managing the device still make sense? The fact that the worker needs access to email, does anyone really care whether the email is on one version of mail software on one device, versus on another email software program on another device?

As long as the user has access to their email, contacts, calendar appointments, and important documents, and the user doesn't care that the interface from one device is different than another, why would I.T. care about the consistency of the application or the device. A more tech savvy user doesn't need their email program on three different devices to look exactly the same, they're fine using multiple tools as long as they have access to their information at anytime from anywhere. What I.T. does care about is that if the employee leaves the organization, that the data is protected or potentially wiped off the devices, so it's about the data, not necessarily about the device or user interface.

Protecting Data, Not the Device

As organizations focus on what is most important to it, the focus is around the security of data. A device, a device's operating system, and the applications on a device are not the critical aspect for control. It's about protecting the data, ensuring that information deemed private or confidential is protected, or information is removed when an employee parts from the organization. So the focus is on the data and how to control access to the data.

A very simple concept is to encrypt the data on the device and tie the encryption to the user's logon account. The only way to access the data is to enter in an appropriate "corporate logon" credential to unencrypt the content. If someone else gains access to the system, unless they have the credential information, they cannot unencrypt the content. If the individual is terminated from the organization, their logon credentials are disabled so that even if they still have the encrypted content sitting on a thumb drive, tablet, phone, or up in a cloud hosted file system, without a valid logon, they cannot enter the credentials needed to unencrypt the content they have stored.

The encryption and decryption is tied to the user's logon, not to the device, not to the operating system, not to any specific application, thus the credentials and the encryption and decryption of content can roam between devices and works whether the content is stored on a local device or up in a cloud service. When the user gets a new device or moves to a different device, their encrypted data is moved to the new device, and their logon credentials (assuming they are still valid) will continue to decrypt and re-encrypt the content. I.T. gets out of the device management business, and can remain focused on enabling business policies and supporting users instead of chasing the never ending proliferation of devices and cloud storage mediums.

As for technologies that provide this level of functionality, since most enterprise workers logon to Microsoft Active Directory, having credentials tied to user A.D. accounts tends to be the standard in enterprise organizations. Within the Microsoft product line, Microsoft has embedded a technology they call Active Directory Rights Management Services (RMS) that provides policy-based content encryption and decryption. RMS has been available for over a decade, however was not a serious contender in enterprise data protection because for most of that decade, Microsoft only supported Windows-based systems with Office-based application protection. However in the past decade, a whole ecosystem has emerged supporting non-Microsoft endpoints such as Macs, iPads, Android devices along with non-Microsoft files like PDF files, TIF and JPG graphic files, and MP3 and WMV media content. And with RMS included as part of the common Microsoft Office 365 "E3" and "E5" licensing that most organizations that use Office 365 own, this technology simply needs to be enabled and the enterprise will have a very sophisticated file-level encryption technology for its employees.

Protection by Automation, Not by Brute Force

Anyone who's raised children knows there's only so much protection one can build around the kids without putting them in a padded bubble, that the best a parent can do is educate their children, help them make good decisions, and make security and protection part of a day-to-day process. The same is true for the workforce, that multiple levels of automation and education can provide a better enforcement of policies and security than putting up barriers and attempting to brute force manage the protection of data and systems.

For the past decade, I.T. organizations have built up protective walls with network firewalls, locked down systems, and protection devices on everything within the datacenter, however as users have needed an ability to share information with others outside of the organization, because the internal systems are so locked down, users have just gone around I.T. and setup their own file sharing and content collaboration sites without I.T.'s knowledge. Security assessments of these organizations typically find a very tightly managed environment along with a completely unmanaged and completely unsecure side of the operations.

As organizations loosen their security grips, provide I.T. supported methods of sharing information and communicating, both internally and externally, with automation tools that automatically encrypt secured content, with a little end user education, these organizations have better overall security in the enterprise.

Taking the model of protecting and encrypting data, organizations that set filters on data stores, filters on email transports, and filters on upload and download streams, can automatically intercept content and encrypt content in transit as well as at rest. Rather than depending on the user to think about encrypting content, content is automatically categorized, encrypted, and tied to user's credentials. As documents and messages are then moved to other devices, stored in external file sharing sites, or copied to USB thumb drives, the information is encrypted and can only be opened by authorized individuals in the organization. If the content is shared with someone, that recipient must be given explicit access to the content by the document owner. If the content is accidentally saved in a public site or a device is stolen, the only individuals that can decrypt the content are those with authorized credentials. If the individual is terminated, their access to

29

any and all information is disabled.

So the change is from trying to state that data can only be stored on in-house protected systems that we all know the content will be attached and sent/saved anyway, to a process where the expectation is that all data will get out of the organization. Therefore, automating the categorization and encryption of the content to protect it from unauthorized access provides organizations a better method of enterprise security.

Monitoring to Ensure Security Protection is Working

Even the best designed and implemented security system is prone to compromise, either through malicious access, or by accidental breach. As organizations automate systems in an attempt to simplify unwanted access to information, having the ability to monitor and test content access on a regular basis ensures that security automation is working as expected.

If the organization is automating the encryption of content and testing to ensure that content is properly being encrypted both at rest and in transit, the organization can validate that content is being protected as expected. Additionally, a process of validating that only those authorized to access content remains enforced, ensures that even if someone who is not authorized to access content cannot access the content as expected.

The organization wants to validate that information stored outside of the organization is properly protected, which would include periodic checks of secured content on employee owned devices, content stored in cloud hosted environments, content copied down to USB thumb drives, and the like.

As security shifts from protecting devices to protecting data, an organization's security personnel just has to follow the trail of data to ensure that the data the organization wants to protect is indeed being protected.

Making Way for I.T. Enablers

As more and more users become tech savvy, and the reliance solely on the I.T. expert diminishes, the I.T. technologist needs to make way for a rising role of the I.T. enabler. The I.T. enabler may not even be in the I.T. department, but could be a marketing specialist, or a business analyst, or data analyst on the frontline of the organization. If data and core applications reside in the cloud, and the consumer of the data is working from their personal tablet from home, what role does the I.T. department's personnel play in the value it provides to that individual?

It's a far different perspective than the model of the past where the consumer of data worked on a company owned desktop, sat within the corporate office, connected to the corporate backbone, and accessed data sitting on a corporate owner server. And if this data consumer is accessing critical business data, generating valuable reports, working up business models to drastically increase the revenues of the organization and/or save the organization a significant amount of money, that individual has an extremely strategic role in the organization.

This is the changing face of I.T. and how the distribution of knowledge and the enablement of external sources will forever change the role I.T. has in an organization.

Facilitating Supply from I.T.

I.T.'s role in the new world environment shifts from the controller of information and systems, to one where I.T. facilitates supply to meet demand in a secured and automated manner. Similar to the days where the important person in the village was the one that dug the well and made the aqueducts to bring water to the city, today it's the person running the water treatment plant that watches dials and makes sure the right valves are turned on to ensure water continuously flows to meet the demands of its consumers. I.T. will play an even more important role here and into the future because when I.T. is doing their job right, the users in the organization will have access to the data they want, when they want it, from any device they're using, and the user will never have to worry whether the content is secured, protected, backed up, and properly managed. It'll take as much, if not more work and planning to make I.T. work right in the new world of I.T., but from a completely different manner of operations than in the past.

The I.T. landscape is much broader today with data on a multitude of devices and stored not only on corporate owned and managed systems, but on employee owned systems as well as content stored in the public cloud. I.T.'s role has expanded, but in the transition to the new world environment, I.T. has to do things very differently than in the past. The new model with old processes and systems won't work. There's a need for distinct changes in storage, management, protection, control, and automation that will allow I.T. to be the enabler for an enterprise and play a critical role in the overall business success of the enterprise.

5 EMBRACING THE NEW MODEL OF ROLLING UPDATES

Initial cloud migration focus has been simply migrating applications and services to the cloud, however the cloud introduces new models in application updates and operational changes that are different than what organizations have been used to. Instead of a 3-7 year major update cycles, cloud-based solutions typically continuously update features and functions on an ongoing basis. And not just rolling upgrades and updates on the backend cloud systems, but changes to endpoint client applications like in Windows 10 or Microsoft Office 2016 have brought rolling updates right to the fingertips of employees.

Experiencing Updates to Cloud-hosted Applications

In 2016 alone, there were over 200 new updates rolled into the Microsoft Office 365 product line, and over 350 new updates to Microsoft's Azure cloud environment. Similar product updates were injected into other cloud services by Amazon, Google, Box.com, Salesforce, and others. Most backend feature updates are added as new modules, so those updates usually aren't too visible to users unless the users specifically logon to the application portal and click on the new added application, or the user installs a new App that enables this new backend functionality.

It is up to the user, and many times the administrator, to "enable" much of the added functionality such as Microsoft Teams, Microsoft Planner, the new Office 365 Compliance and Discovery Center, and the like.

Experiencing User Application Updates

However for client facing applications like Microsoft Office 2016, Windows 10, Box.com and Salesforce.com apps, actual new features and functions are added right into the application and user interface that users access every day. These are features and changes that show up when an app is updated, which in some cases the updates occur monthly.

Some add features are like backend services additions that unless an employee actually "clicks" on the new feature, it really doesn't change the way the user does things. However the more disruptive changes are when a function is removed from an application. This deprecation of features doesn't happen too often, however every vendor has been guilty of removing functionality they deem as non-essential, or replace a feature with something the vendor believes is "better," this is when rolling updates become a challenge for organizations.

A decade ago, organizations would spend weeks and months vetting a product before they roll out the update throughout the enterprise, ensuring that the new version was 100% accepted by all users. However that model of full acceptance was exactly why it took 3, 5, 7 years before an organization would upgrade to an updated version of an application. In many instances, an entire enterprise would be held back from the functionality of a new application because a handful of users would be inconvenienced by a change in functionality of the new application.

While one would think it would be important to ensure 100% acceptance, the problem was for the users that wanted and needed the new functionality and had to "wait", those users would frequently go out and buy a 3rd party plug-in to the "old" application to meet their needs. It is these 3rd party plug-ins and workarounds that further complicated upgrades now that those customizations required application compatibility testing before the enterprise could move forward.

This vicious cycle of 100% acceptance created years of painful migration cycles for everyone, whereas the experience has been the rolling updates, while temporarily disruptive for a few for a short period of time, the underlying benefit achieved by all employees with improved functionality actually results in better experiences in the long run for enterprises.

Understanding User Perspective on Rolling Updates

The impact of rolling updates has actually been well received by the end user community. Users are very familiar with frequent update cycles as they've gotten to accept them on their iPhones, iPads, Android devices, Apple Macs, and other systems where the core operating system and apps have regularly released updates.

When asked whether they want to be working on an old 5-10 year old system, or have an up to date system and application experience, users overwhelmingly prefer a more modern experience. Even users who may seem to be against frequent updates and changes brought on by rolling updates of their desktop or laptop system, they're typically users that have the latest mobile phone and tablet system, and they've been adaptive to the frequent changes they've seen on their mobile devices, and are more receptive to rolling changes on their business systems than may otherwise be perceived.

Supporting the Tech Savvy Workforce

One of the reasons the rolling updates have been better received by the general workforce is the fact that the workforce is more tech savvy. Whether it is the newer entrants to the workforce that were born into a world of devices and the Internet, or the more senior workforce that have now been working on computers and systems for 2-3 decades, the fact is that users are no longer neophytes of technology.

Of course there are always a handful of individuals that prefer consistency and are slower to adapt change than others, however holding back an entire enterprise from the reality of evolving tech puts organizations at a disadvantage when competitors are leveraging modern technical solutions, and attracting bright new entrants to the workforce that can leverage the capabilities available in the latest technical solutions and services.

Supporting the Workforce in an Evolving Work Environment Model

Organizations have found that when they provide their users with current tools, employees figure out how to use them and leverage them to do things their predecessors were unable to do with the tools from a decade or two ago. Additionally, rolling updates typically embed new features and functions that in the past organizations had to go out and buy 3rd party plug-ins or entire add-on products to get a job done. Instead of buying 4-5 tools, mainstream applications are embedded and integrating key functionality of these various tools into a single suite of products that out of the box provides integration between various components, and assure supportability of integration since they are bundled as an integrated suite of tools

Organizations have also found that the effort of spending 2-3 years to assess a new (major) release of a product for 100% supportability across the enterprise is extremely costly. By embracing rolling updates, I.T. organizations instead spend their time and effort simply helping the handful of employees that need extra assistance when a new feature or function is rolled out. It's been an 80/20 rule (or more like 98/2 rule) where 80-98% of the users have no problems at all with rolling updates, and the 2%-3% of the users that do need support can get assistance when they need it. Over time, I.T. organizations have found the percentage of users needing assistance after an update is rolled out drops dramatically as users learn to adapt to changes, and just like ongoing mobile phone and tablet updates, just get into a rhythm of figuring stuff out as they go.

Addressing Regulated Industries That Require Application Consistency

There are several industries where consistency of an application is a requirement for the approved compliance and acceptance of a specific process or procedure. What has been experienced in the past 6-9 months are auditors that are more accepting of variations of applications in regulated processes. Compliance auditors have found there's more risk to the organization with 5-10 year old unsupported and insecure applications, than the risk an updated version of an application poses on the consistency of test results. While a data acquisition device needs to measure consistent results over time, a Web browser or a Word processor used to view the results or generate reports has NO impact on the test data itself. Auditors too have become more tech savvy, and are more clearly understanding when static application systems have (or don't have) an impact on test results and acquired data.

And for organizations that have isolated cases where regulated systems cannot be rolled forward with new versions of applications, those systems can remain on an older version of software, and the other 99% of the enterprise can roll forward with the latest release. Typically the highly-regulated systems are completely isolated from the enterprise anyway with little or no integration to day to day users, so holding back an entire enterprise from upgrading and updating their systems makes little sense when isolated and regulated systems can very easily co-exist in the enterprise for the dedicated usage as needed.

Distributing Support to Experts Throughout the Enterprise

And a best practice enjoyed by organizations that have advanced their support for rolling updated applications have leveraged the process where support is distributed to non-IT individuals who are tech savvy and can supplement I.T. helpdesk to support the user community. Every organization has peer experts that enjoy working with technologies and share their knowledge and experience with others that reside outside of the traditional I.T. department and helpdesk organization. Leveraging these subject matter experts (SMEs) and even embracing them as an extension of the organization's support workforce provides a great mechanism to address dynamic updates throughout the enterprise.

Many I.T. departments have formally added these distributed SMEs to knowledge sharing distribution lists and support portals so they can share their experiences, and have access to the latest shared information from others throughout the organization working with end users. The SMEs don't mind adding a task to their daily responsibilities when they may have access to early adopter trainings, pre-release programs, access to SME knowledge groups, and just have something different in their days to do and to experience.

6 SIMPLIFYING APPLICATION INTEGRATION WITH COMPREHENSIVE SUITES

As has been shared in previous chapters of this book is one of the big challenges for organizations in the past has been the reliance on old applications, with multiple 3rd party add-ins that tended to break any time a new update for any of the core products or plug-ins were changed. As new products are evolving with updated features and functions, there's less of a need for 3rd party plug-ins, and fewer problems as updates for the products are released.

Shifting Away from Best of Breed to Integrated Suites

Organizations have found that when their email, Web conferencing, Video conferencing, contact management, telephony, and document collaboration applications all come from the same vendor in a unified suite, when new features or functions are released, there's assurances the new updates will work with all of the other components within the suite. This is not necessarily true when there are 10 different products, from 10 different vendors that are integrated together where staggered upgrades and updates tend to break one component or another.

For many years, it was to the organization's benefit of having a best of breed selection of technologies when various vendors had solutions that uniquely did something that another solution lacked, however these days, most products are very similar to one another. Mainstream applications these days support multiple platforms (Windows, Mac, iOS and Android mobile devices, Linux, etc), and most applications have identical features and functions. And with the rolling update process for applications, an organization doesn't have to wait 3-5 years before a feature is added, typically within a few weeks, the products leapfrog other solutions to include similar features and more features than their competitors.

The key has been to embrace vendors with deep pockets that are constantly investing in Research and Development, and including new features and rolling updates to their products. It goes back to the "rolling updates" conversation that it behooves an organization to embrace a vendor that has frequent updates, and to accept those updates as the business benefit that they are. In both the short term and in the long run, the adoption of new solutions addresses and solves problems that got enterprises caught up in the lengthy upgrade and update process that ultimately caused more problems than they ended up solving.

Handling Situations Where Customization is Required

Along the same line of thinking, while rolling updates of integrated suites minimizes the effort and challenges organizations have in utilizing the latest features and functions available to users, the fewer customizations and fewer integration points the product has also minimizes potential issues during the rolling update process. As much as customizations can make a user's experience nicer or better, the customizations can also create a hook that gets broken the next time the application rolls in with an update. In the end, the thing that makes the experience easier and better for users is the thing that creates the biggest problems for users down the line.

Using the Southwest Airlines analogy usually clarifies this experience. Southwest Airlines has repeatedly been the most profitable and most on time airline in the industry because of standardization. They have adopted the Boeing 737 plane as their fleet standard, enabling the interchange of parts, planes, pilots, and galley carts throughout their network of flights. If a plane is broken, they have common replacement parts, minimizing their need to inventory unique parts across their service centers. If a plane is delayed, they can steal another plane that is of identical configuration and move pilots (all certified on the same 737 configuration) to what fits the needs of the organization. Their flight crews and their customers know exactly where to find things and what to expect onboard because of the uniformity across planes.

There have been Boeing 737 recalls that have caused Southwest Airlines to ground 60-70% of its fleet all at the same time, however in all cases, they've been able to rotate in planes for servicing to minimize impact to less than a few hours fleet wide. While they could minimize the impact by having multiple makes and models of planes, the challenges other airlines have in having broken planes in airports without parts, airplanes stranded in locations without certified pilots, having plane recalls that may only impact 10% of the fleet but requiring days to rotate the right service technicians to the right location, to service the specific issue grounds the fleet longer because of the "thought" that distributing risk was better for the organization.

Customization in I.T. systems was important in early days of technology when users were less tech savvy, and directing the users to specific features, functions, or information was critical. Back in the day when the icons on a desktop or menu items on the Start Bar had to be in the exact same place, otherwise users couldn't launch an application are a thing of the past. A more tech savvy workforce, along with a distribution of subject matter experts throughout an enterprise can overcome the need for absolute idiot-proof customization that is a root cause of many rolling update changes.

Accepting Sporadic Downtime

There is a re-education factor in this new world of thinking, that sporadic download caused by an incident is better than the prolonged upgrade processes and ongoing backwardness of the past. No one wants downtime, and downtime during a critical period could be debilitating, but just as Southwest Airlines overcomes recall challenges that brings down their entire fleet, the recovery time for the organization and the sheer benefit of being able to leverage the latest business functionality actually does outweigh the perceived disadvantages.

An organization can complain it'll lose "millions of dollars" during an outage, yet willing to spend tens of millions of dollars doing things that simply schedules the downtime and ongoing cripples the business as it tries to control the risk. It's hard to argue that the most consistently profitable airline is doing something wrong in their risk mitigation that other airlines that distribute their risk are doing something better.

Modernize Applications to Minimize Integration Challenges

Another by-product of keeping applications up to date with the latest release is that the application to application integration tends to work better across modern apps, than across very old applications. Application vendors add in functionality in their rolling updates to fix problems of integration between various applications, so many times the solution to fix a problem is to update the application itself.

It is these changes in norms and best practices that change what I.T. organizations have grown to believe are requirements to overcome challenges and limitations, and rolling into the new world of application management becomes the solution to everyday problems.

Falling Back to On-Premise Solutions

When all else fails where an application HAS to remain the same version, the organization can choose to retain the older application as a separate path for upgrades and updates than the rest of the organization. The entire organization doesn't need to sink to the lowest common denominator for application versioning and support.

An application can remain on-premise, can remain on a several year old version, and retain identical archaic configurations if need be. Even a simple variation like migrating the isolated application as a Virtual Machine and running the application in a hosted cloud environment could enable an organization to get rid of on-premise resources, leverage the cloud, but retain all other features, functions, and operations to retain version and update controls.

There are several different options for organizations, but the mindset that the organization that moves forward in its operations can benefit from ongoing advantages in allowing the workforce to utilize the latest releases of applications and services available.

Part III:
Realigning I.T. in the New World of Cloud Computing

7 SPRING CLEANING OF THE DATACENTER(S)

As organizations modernize their applications and migrate applications and servers to the cloud, it is important that the organization "cleans up" their on-premise environment to begin the process of minimizing I.T.'s operational footprint. Many organizations power down old servers and virtual machines, but months (years) later they're still taking up space in racks, storage systems, being backed up nightly, retaining the same footprint before the services were migrated out of the datacenter.

The way organizations realize savings from shifting services out of their datacenter is to eliminate unused systems and equipment. It is this clean-up that helps organizations truly see the minimization of their datacenters brought on by their cloud migration efforts.

Identifying Unused Servers and Resources

There are several ways to uncover unused systems, a good starting point is to look at the services that were migrated to the cloud such as email servers, fileservers, and associated systems like archiving servers, journaling servers, and gateways. Additionally, servers that were associated with migrated applications like anti-virus and anti-spam servers or appliances, relay servers, and the like should also be assessed for elimination. Other options of uncovering unused resources is to check the log files of systems to determine if anyone has logged on or used the systems in the past month or two. And all else fails, a quick and simple way of determining whether anyone uses a system that is suspected to not be in use is simply unplugging the system from the network and wait until someone complains.

Consolidating Underutilized Servers and Resources

In addition to unused systems are systems that are underutilized. Virtual host servers (VMware and Hyper-V hosts) that once hosted 8-10 active guest sessions may only have 2-3 systems running on them after application servers (email, filesharing, telephony, etc) were decommissioned. Since the host systems had the capacity to run 8-10 systems at one point, consolidating 3-4 hosts each with 2-3 virtual machines running on them can decrease host servers from 3-4 hosts underutilized host systems down to 1 host system.

Host consolidation opens up hardware to be repurposed for other uses, or older hosts (or host systems that are having reliability problems) can be swapped out with idle or underutilized systems, and the older hardware can be retired or resold on the secondary market to capture back funds.

Many organizations miss the opportunity to cash in on unused hardware, that while the equipment may only capture 20 or 30 cents on a dollar of the original purchase price, it' still better than just having the systems run unused and idle, taking up electrical power, rack space, and require administrative overhead when the collection of 20-30% of the original value is still cash in hand for the organization.

Decommissioning Unused Servers and Systems

Organizations many times have a hard time shutting down systems wondering if the system serves a purpose that might create a problem if the system is removed. As previously mentioned, a simple solution to that is simply disconnect the server from the network for a few days and see if anything stops working. If all of a sudden something critical stops working, you can simply plug the server back into the network. However if after a few days nothing has failed, the server can be targeted for decommissioning and removed from the network.

Server removal many times is more than just powering off a system and/or deleting the virtual machine that was running. Many times a formal "uninstall" procedure is needed to back out a server from the network. If a server is a node of a larger environment, or participated in some type of replication or routing, the uninstall or formal decommissioning process is advised. In many cases it is just running an uninstall (or install /u) type of command to remove the system, validating the appropriate process of server removal is always advised.

Beyond powering off a system or uninstalling the system from software perspective, the physical removal of hardware out of racks, or the deletion of the virtual machine and any associated storage once taken up by the application is the true elimination of the system from the network. If you are unsure whether the data on the system may be necessary at some point, backup the system to tape, mark the tape, and put the tape on a shelf so you can remove the server and/or delete all storage remnants of the system. Leaving racks of hardware, and terabytes of storage remain idle because of the lack of knowledge whether the system can be eliminated just takes up space and costs the organization money for the idle storage of unused systems.

Eliminating Support Systems and Resources

Once core systems have been eliminated from racks and virtual machine images have been deleted and completely eliminated from the datacenter, a sweep across the environment for patching servers, monitoring servers, clusters or disaster recovery replicas need to be searched out and either eliminated or at a minimum diminished.

An organization with 1000 servers may have had 200 servers running for management and support. However when the organization is now down to 500 servers, the organization does not still need 200 management and support systems. It's this proportional elimination of support systems that will further decrease the footprint of the datacenter, and help the organization shrink the number of virtual machines, host servers, appliances, and racks from their datacenter.

8 REASSESSING THE NEW NORM DATACENTER ENVIRONMENT

With an initial round of servers and systems eliminated from the environment, and hopefully some consolidation of resources to newer or more robust systems, the I.T. team now has a better idea of the current I.T. footprint. The next step is to reassess the new norm for the organization that includes how the organization should manage what's left in the datacenter, and how the organization can further minimize the on-premise footprint of its I.T. operations.

Reassessing the I.T. Needs of the Organization

While in the previous chapter we merely removed systems that were not in use, this step is to do a more active look at the resulting I.T. needs of the organization. For many organizations at this juncture, email and file sharing have been moved to the cloud, as has other key business applications like the organization's Intranet, www server, and potentially accounting/ERP system and telephony.

If the organization has moved virtually everything to the cloud at this point, then there may just be the organization's Active Directory and a handful of legacy management systems still residing in the datacenter. Other organizations may find a handful of legacy server applications that were not moved to SaaS or cloud-based VMs because of a lack of cloud support for the applications, or the need for the organization to truly internalize the management and operations of the existing system(s) on-premise.

With a final reassessment of the resulting systems, the organization can determine whether additional applications can be modernized and removed out of the datacenter, consolidated with other applications that exist in the enterprise, encapsulate the remaining systems and move them out as hosted virtual machines in the cloud, or consolidate and retain the resulting systems into a handful of host servers or racks in the datacenter as needed.

Confirming that Business Needs are Being Fulfilled

With the datacenter for the most part cleaned up, this is a good time to determine whether there are simple things that I.T. could be doing to add services at this time. This may be going back to old I.T. plans to find those things that I.T. never got around to doing in the past because of a lack of time or there wasn't budget to buy hardware that was needed to run the application.

Now that many applications have likely been eliminated from the datacenters, organizations find there is excess capacity (servers, storage, network bandwidth, and I.T. time) to verify if an old project is still relevant for I.T. to spin up.

Architecting for a Small I.T. Datacenter Footprint

By now, I.T. will have modernized the existing application and datacenter environment, removed all unused systems and appliances, deleted unnecessary storage and archives, and added any previously lingering applications and services. So the next step is to formally re-architect an appropriate I.T. environment for "what's left."

And rather than simply downsizing existing systems, the focus should be to consider replacement services that are appropriate for the current I.T. environment. As an example, if the organization had an enterprise class monitoring system with 30 servers around the globe, rather than cutting that back to say 5 servers, to instead sit down and determine if there might be a monitoring solution that is more appropriate for an I.T. operations of the current size and scope of the enterprise's now existing environment. It may be determined that a cloud-based monitoring solution can completely replace the legacy environment, or that a solution that will run on just 2 servers could fulfill the current needs of the organization.

The same thought process is applied to the patching and server management platform, whether the organization still needs an enterprise class management system when 80% of the servers are no longer within the walls of the organization's datacenter and 50% of the applications are SaaS-based that require no patching and management. It's a complete zero-based assessment of what is appropriate for the organization given the current modernized environment.

Another area that is common for review are Active Directory domain controllers, that most organizations have several throughout the enterprise. With fewer servers and more users and devices authenticating over mobile devices, the need for several domain controllers in the datacenter or throughout each site is an old design. Additionally, 64-bit server technology over the past decade now enables thousands (tens of thousands) of users to successfully authenticate to a single domain controller, so an Active Directory architecture based on Windows NT designs from 20-years ago can be rethought and realigned to the organization's current needs.

One option for directory authentication that is covered in Chapter 11 of this book is looking to move the entire Active Directory infrastructure into the Microsoft Azure cloud. Microsoft now has a service called Azure Active Directory Domain Services that requires no "servers", is a cloud-based service that allows devices (and more than just Windows devices) to "join" and be managed by the Azure ADDS, push policies to the authenticated systems, and effectively be Active Directory as a service.

Rethinking the datacenter architecture is a ground-up approach of reassessing what the organization now has in on-premise applications versus cloud-based applications, new ways of addressing remaining services like monitoring, authentication, and management, and building up an environment that fulfills on the current needs of the enterprise.

9 THE RISE OF IDENTIFY, ALIGN, AND SUPPLY

With the changing nature from a Plan, Build, Run model to an Identify, Align, and Supply model, this chapter focuses on the changing nature of I.T. management and I.T. personnel that will be managing and maintaining this new world of the modern I.T. environment.

The Decline of the Buy, Build, and Run Model

With the better part of three decades of I.T. experience in buying, building, and running I.T., changing to a new model has been, is, and will be a challenge for I.T. organizations. It takes a complete new rethinking of I.T. to embrace the fact that I.T. is different these days, which requires a change in management and support models.

I.T. organizations no longer spend weeks or months buying and building hardware systems. Entire groups of I.T. personnel are no longer needed to rack and stack equipment, and watch blinking lights to make sure hardware systems are running. Processes like replacing backup tapes, monitoring system queues, restarting system services, or rebooting servers are no longer the daily tasks of I.T. organizations that have their applications in a SaaS or PaaS based model. Even the ongoing process of planning and performing system maintenance, updates, and upgrades are eliminated from the job responsibilities of I.T. personnel.

This doesn't mean that I.T. employees are out of a job though. As much as many mundane tasks have been eliminated from an organization, the evolution of I.T. in a cloud-optimized environment refocuses the tasks of I.T. personnel to proactive points of responsibilities that benefit the organization in improving security, optimizing employee use, and leveraging data to provide improved business services, and decreasing the cost and overhead typically associated with I.T. operations.

Focusing on Customization of PaaS Model Applications

One focus for I.T. personnel is shifting IaaS-based applications from running on virtual machines to PaaS or SaaS based applications. As has been described previously, IaaS is not a very efficient model since it requires patching, updating, and traditional I.T. management that organizations really want to eliminate from the I.T. tasks to optimize I.T. operations. Shifting to PaaS or SaaS applications accomplishes this.

I.T. management have allocated time for personnel to assess all running IaaS systems and determine what can be done to shift the applications away from running on virtual machines to running as services. With the identification of systems that could be prioritized for conversion, I.T. can then create a roadmap and spend weeks or months simply stepping through the process of optimizing applications into a more efficient and effective runtime model. This modernization effort could keep I.T. busy for a very long time.

Even after applications have been migrated off IaaS to a PaaS-based model, the continual customization of the application, the optimization of the PaaS-application, and even adding in new features and functions identified during the application suitability step on what will make an application more effective for employees becomes a series of valuable tasks for I.T. to perform.

Shifting to a Services Model in I.T.

As organizations start to "buy" their services from cloud providers, they shift away from a product deployment model to a services consumption model. The organization no longer needs to size servers, build systems, configure fault tolerance, plan for datacenter space, buy equipment, burn in hardware, and train administrators on backup and maintenance tasks. As a buyer of services, the requirement is no longer to plan the build and implementation of technologies, but rather to purchase the appropriate amount of capacity, and train users to use the application.

There's still a very important requirement to plan, prepare, and train users on the consumption of the services, but it's more end user experience focused than the past of building highly available and reliable systems. The building of the "backend systems" is no longer in the control of the buyer. If a certain level of service are required, then the organization needs to assess the capability of the cloud service provider in meeting those requirements. However in many cases, you get what you get, and you just have to choose to take what the service provider provides now and hope the provider will upgrade their services in the future. As cloud providers seek to maintain customers and offer competitive solutions, they are incented to upgrade their service offerings, so the cloud-based solutions have proven to get better over time.

Supply and Demand Become Key

As a consumer of services, the important factor is matching the supply and demand. While some providers charge a flat rate for what most organizations would feel is acceptable service capacity for each user, such as with email messaging, some services are purchased based on demand and usage. If users are used to unlimited supply, they can consume the service in a manner that causes an unnecessary burden of expense. It's similar to a case where if electricity and water were at a flat rate, no one would turn off the lights around the house and everyone would take extra-long showers as there would be no negative consequence to the user. In these cases, the service would be abused. Some I.T. services, like storage of information, is charged per gigabyte and terabyte, so from a cost perspective it behooves an organization to only store information that is needed, and eliminate content that is not. Or if virtual machines are charged when they are running, but not charged when they are stopped, in test and development environments where dozens of virtual machines are used for testing, the organization needs to turn off test/dev systems that aren't in use.

As every economics student learns in school, it is when supply equals demand where cost optimization is achieved. And with lower demand, the consumption is conserved, and costs are driven further down in the organization. As the organization subscribes for services, having methods to optimize the desired capacity for demand will help the organization pay for only the capacity the organization requires.

Identifying the Needs of the Organization

To come up with the appropriate amount of capacity, the I.T. department needs to shift its architecture planning from capacity planning in terms of how many servers are needed, to planning capacity by identifying the appropriate amount of supply that is needed to fulfill on the organization's demand for resources. And instead of simply looking at what the organization has in use today and the current growth in usage space, the organization needs to do real assessments on requirements and demand.

When capacity was seen as "free" to the users, they may have stored everything, saved everything, or configured more test systems than what was really needed, because stuff was cheap or free in the past. Thus in a "pay for use" model, usage needs to be optimized, and systems put in place to help regulate consumption to an appropriate level.

This process of identifying the needs of the organization is best done by a business analyst who can assess what users within the organization do, how information, data, and I.T. services are used, stored, and consumed. In order for I.T. to be more effective in a consumption model environment, I.T. needs to better understand the business. And more than just what departments do within the organization, also what an optimized department would do if it maximized its capability of I.T. So the goal is to take the best practices of the best organizations around, and leverage and optimize those best practices to use as the baseline for capacity analysis and planning.

Interview and Observations more than Architecture and Design

The identification process of the new optimized I.T. environment is helped by interviews and observations within the business. Instead of an I.T. architect and designer attending I.T. technology conferences and designing server capacity, I.T. systems fault tolerance, and compliance security in a conference room, to truly build I.T. in the new world, the I.T. designer, or more appropriately a business analyst, needs to get inside the business and understand the tasks performed by employees of the organization.

By observing how sales people sell, how manufacturing is run, how marketing is driven, how paperwork is processed within an organization, and how similar businesses do it better, the I.T. analyst better understands true business processes. A good example is a salesperson who might traditionally sit behind a desktop making phone calls all day may not be a good example of what the salesperson COULD do if the person wasn't stuck "behind" a fixed desktop PC system of 2 decades ago. Instead, a salesperson could potentially leverage the tools and resources of today in terms of gathering data about sales leads and opportunities by accessing databases and being mobile to actually go "see" how his potential clients do business. By having a mobile device with mobile data analysis tools, a salesperson could be more effective in understanding their clients and thus establishing new business relationship and generate new revenues for the organization.

It is this use of interviews and observations, combined with an understanding of what other organizations do in optimizing and leveraging I.T. that helps an organization better plan for the consumption of services in the future of the business, not based on stale data of the past.

Aligning Business Needs to Success Criteria

Also in terms of I.T. planning, beyond understanding what people within the organization do (or should do) day in and day out, understanding the business and goals of the leaders of the organization is a huge factor in developing success criteria for I.T. services. If the CEO has stated the organization will grow by 40%, then the I.T. growth plan isn't simply taking what the organization is doing today and adding 40% in budgeting and estimating the future of I.T., but rather determine how the organization can grow by 40% but increase I.T. costs by significantly less than 40%. Again, instead of the old model of giving each salesperson a cubical tied to a network wired personal desktop computer and plug in phone, what if the 40% growth in business can be achieved with 0 growth in office space by providing employees mobility of their I.T. supplied tools and resources.

The salesperson with a mobile device, wireless connectivity, and telephony on the go can allow that additional hire to be anywhere and get their job done. The person may still need a cubicle to work from, but instead of fixed offices where each person gets their own office with their own dedicated PC, the organization can have shared offices where individuals can bring their mobile device into the office and connect wirelessly to the enterprise. This flexibility in workforce workspace can potentially allow an organization to consolidate dedicated office space into shared spaces thus allowing for the growth of the organization, without the linear growth in cost.

Similarly, if the Board of Directors set the direction for the business to add services on another continent, again, the business model could be take what I.T. has today in terms of "servers" and "racks" and "routers" and "desktop systems" and replicate a current office to an overseas office, OR I.T. could leverage stretched networking capabilities or even cloud-based services so that a new office can be setup with NO on premise services, NO physical writing and just mobile devices for users. I.T. can just drop in a wireless access point to a new site that connects back to an Internet connection that gives the users in the office full access to all I.T. resources in another existing datacenter or to cloud service providers.

I.T. can align its services best when it rethinks its role, and prepares its services to fulfill on the needs of the business, not on the monolithic cookie-cutter replication of I.T. systems and services of the past. With this thinking, I.T. can be an enabler of business growth with less of a burden on the linear costs of growth and business success.

Identifying Service Needs and Requirements

With an understanding of the goals and initiatives of the business from top down, and knowing what individuals within the organization do day in and day out, I.T. can now identify the service needs and requirements of the employees of the organization. If users can untether themselves from a desk and be more mobile, then I.T. can provide mobile services instead of desk side services. If users have historically saved everything and used whatever capacity was available, I.T. could better optimize storage and usage demands through automated throttles and information management filters to more effectively implement a service level that more appropriately meets the needs and requirements of the organization.

Buy versus Build

The cloud is not the pinnacle of success for organizations where every workload in the organization needs to be hosted in the cloud, but rather the cloud should be seen as just one additional option the organization can choose to select in their I.T. fulfillment plans. As early adopters to the cloud found, just because cloud services were available early on didn't mean they were reliable enough for the organization, feature rich enough to meet the daily needs of employees, or economical enough to make sense for the organization. With proper strategy planning and a good understanding of the needs of the business, an organization can better determine whether cloud services should be bought on a consumption basis, or whether the organization should build capacity as it has done so for years.

By focusing on what is best to fulfill the needs of users, the decision to buy versus build capacity makes more sense. If users need to spin up virtual machines at a rate of dozens or hundreds a day, it may very well be cheaper to build a series of traditional server farms to manage the demand in capacity that to buy services from a cloud provider. However if an organization's development department requires system capacity for sporadic use, and the systems can be shut down when not in use, the organization can leverage the "agility" of the cloud by buying limited services on demand as needed and pay for those services as used.

A new thing organizations also need to add to their thinking about the cloud is whether an all or nothing approach makes sense when making buy versus build decisions. If 80% of the users can move their development to cloud services, yet for 20% of the users it makes more sense to use in-house development resources, the organization doesn't need to have just a single strategy. Having this flexibility in thinking can allow the organization to best optimize cloud benefits, potentially even a hybrid approach, that makes the most sense for the organization.

Conversely though, if the organization uses the removal of on premise resources as a deciding factor for cost cutting, yet the organization chooses a "hybrid model" where it remains both on premise and consumes services from the cloud, the organization may find that the decrease in cost it was expecting is not as low as projected, and actually may increase if a hybrid model is chosen. If the organization has to continue to buy and manage servers, licenses, and other resources to retain a "footprint" on premise, the cost associated with the on-premise resources plus the monthly cost of the cloud resources might increase the overall cost of services.

It's a mathematical calculation that is best done with facts, not with gut feel. Too many I.T. personnel quickly dismiss one model versus another without quantifying what it means to be in one model versus the other for operations. Take email for example, if the organization has 8 email servers today, but chooses to do a split hybrid model where some users will remain on premise and everyone else will be migrated to the cloud, while the organization will still have to pay for the cost of on premise resources, if the organization goes from managing and supporting 8 systems across 3 continents for 4000 users to having 3500 users in the cloud and paying monthly for those users, and drop on premise services down to just 1 system in 1 location, there most certainly is a decrease in maintenance and operational cost of on premise services. While it would likely be cheaper to move everyone to the cloud, there is likely a cost savings by moving most users to the cloud, and hosting just a single on premise system. Do the math to determine the true cost of build versus buy for the organization in decision making.

Optimizing Supply to Demands

As the organization best understands what its employees do, what employees in best run organizations do, and then do some number crunching on various models for build versus buy, the organization can optimize supply to demand. The organization definitely wants to minimize its over purchase of supply if it doesn't use the capacity purchased, and the organization can be more efficient by monitoring and managing user capacity demand and usage, and change practices that can help the organization best optimize costs.

10 REASSESSING THE ROLE OF I.T. IN THE NEW CLOUD MODEL

With a smaller I.T. datacenter footprint, and more apps that are hosted or cloud-managed, a reassessment of I.T. in general and the role of I.T. personnel is likely prudent at this time.

Assessing Personnel Roles in the New I.T. Environment

As the world of I.T. changes from a solely build model to a model where some (or all) I.T. services are purchased as services, the skillsets of the personnel that make up the I.T. operations also needs to change. For some organizations, management may find individuals can be retrained to fit new roles, whereas other organizations may need to recruit a new line of personnel. It is important for I.T. individuals to keep relevant in their skills beyond technology to contribute to the I.T. model of the future.

I.T. Architects Give Way to Business Analysts

As has been noted previously in this book, the role of the I.T. architect changes from a technologist designing servers, system fault tolerance, and software migrations to business analysts who understand the business and the role of employees within the organization. The I.T. architect may still be the same individual fulfilling the role, but the focus is to truly understand the organization, how the business runs, what the business goals and objectives are, and then "designing" the use of technology within the business to fulfill the needs of the employees in the organization.

Instead of taking current demand and capacity and creating models on the size, redundancy, and scalability of systems, it's identifying the applications users need to run and determine what model best fulfills on meeting the needs of the users. The analyst needs to determine whether an application will be hosted by the organization internally, or whether the application can be purchased on a subscription basis from a hosted cloud provider. If a hosted cloud provider doesn't provide the specific application to be run in the cloud, consider a model where the underlying infrastructure (i.e.: virtual machine and OS) is hosted by a cloud provider, and the I.T. organization simply installs and supports the running of the application in the cloud.

The business analyst would also spend a good portion of their time crunching numbers to determine the most effective cost model for the organization. Whether it's paying a flat monthly fee, or whether an "on demand" model leveraging cloud services is appropriate for the organization. As noted in the previous chapter, the costing model is not necessarily a linear monthly cost for cloud hosted applications. Many hosted services can be acquired on a usage basis so that an organization can build capacity to meet peak needs, but shutdown services in the cloud when the capacity is not needed, and thus optimize costs by 40%-60%.

The role of the business analyst in architecting and designing the right I.T. environment is to make sure to "buy" the right capacity to fulfill on the needs of the organization. In this role, it's important to think "outside the box" and not simply take the same application and same business model used today, and just cost the exact same model in the cloud. The cloud is just another input in the cost matrix to use in calculations. The business analyst needs to understand what users in the organization need to do, and then recommend the right application/tool, in the right business model, with the right costing structure to fulfill on the obligation of providing services at the most effective cost and structure.

Technology Upgrade Specialists Give Way to Change Fulfillment Specialists

In the past, I.T. has been focused on upgrading technologies from one version to another. Backend servers were upgraded, and I.T. specialists focused on the upgrade of the server systems. When client applications were upgraded, I.T. specialists focused on deploying applications on user systems. However, in an I.T. environment where applications are provided to users from a centralized hosted environment, there are no backend servers for the organization to upgrade, and frequently no applications to install on end user systems either. The role of I.T. in this transition is to assist in any change fulfillment that needs to be addressed such as user training or integration modifications.

However hosted cloud providers have historically upgraded their systems in real-time, adding in new features and functions, and consumers of the services have had little need for incremental training. The new functionality just appears and is available to the users, and even in major version updates, users have for the most part just "figured out" how the new system works. This goes back to the more tech savvy workforce where users are familiar enough with technologies that they can figure out how to navigate their way around an updated application.

It's the reason the term Change Management is used in the description of this new I.T. role as I.T. won't really have much control to "manage" the change that is happening. Instead, I.T. will just have to fulfill their role in supporting users and the environment when the change occurs.

The individuals fulfilling this role will need less hands-on software imaging and application packaging experience, and be better communicators and support personnel who are able to work through any changes that directly impact business operations. The role focuses on addressing the change and reactively solving any problems, not necessarily handholding users through new features and functions.

Network Administrators Give Way to Supply and Demand Managers

Within I.T. operations, there are a number of different network administrators that oversee various technical functions in the organization. Some administrators oversee databases, others email systems, some provision and deprovision employees, some address security, while others focus on the network infrastructure and storage systems. Some of these roles will remain the same for an organization, at least for a short while, whereas other roles will quickly be replaced.

As an example, if an organization migrates its email system to a hosted cloud environment, there is no need for a role of someone to patch, manage, and update email servers thereafter. In a full cutover of an email system to a hosted cloud environment, there are no remaining on premise email systems to backup, maintain, and manage.

There is however, still a role to administrator email accounts, create email routing policies, address email security rules, and provide end-user support for access to the email system. The role shifts from managing "systems" to effectively administering settings and ensuring that supply and operations meet the needs and demands of the organization.

If an organization moves document storage to the cloud, then the need to manage file systems, storage area network systems, backing up files, and other day to day tasks are eliminated from the organization. However, the organization still has to focus on document management, document change control, security access to content, and things as they relate to user access, modification, and the security of the content.

Some roles are combined as things like email settings or cloud monitoring are sporadic tasks and not particularly full time tasks, so an individual may be responsible for addressing settings for emails, files, stored content, hosted Web servers, and the like. The I.T. role shifts from a specialist in 1 technology platform to someone who needs to be savvy with the administration and management of multiple applications along with the settings and operations of multiple systems.

There's no doubt that as services are shifted to cloud-based environments and even if organizations choose to host applications in-house, that the focus is far less about patching and managing "systems" as once was the responsibility of I.T. specialists. The shift in focus will be about sizing demand, optimizing settings, and ensuring consistent access to the hosted or the on-premise system services.

Help Desk Gives Way to End User Enablement Specialists

A big change organizations will start to see is a shift from traditional "help desk" roles to one of I.T. individuals assisting users to maximize their use of the technologies available to them. As the workplace fills itself with more tech savvy individuals, and organizations broaden their support for various endpoint devices, the organization will find that its need to provide helpdesk support in the traditional sense will change.

The helpdesk individuals will spend less time assisting users to click to open files, or press send to send messages, but rather proactively work with business departments in helping users best leverage the technologies available to them. A frontline support person can greatly contribute to the success of the organization by helping marketing personnel access marketing data and leverage that information to conduct better marketplace assessments. Or sales personnel can be assisted on the frontline to better leverage client support tools, track sales opportunities, increase revenues by better understanding and supporting the end client.

Helpdesk can be shifted from being a reactive support resource helping technically novice individuals with mundane support tasks, to being a group of proactive enablement specialists helping employees be more productive in their day-to-day operations.

Changing Roles Requires New Skills

As with any operational change, the I.T. organization will have different roles in I.T. The skills required in the new world of I.T. is far more business focused and user interaction focused than hands-on technical focused. The make-up of the I.T. department will have fewer individuals running around building, patching, and maintaining systems than in the past, and more individuals doing business assessments, financial and operational optimization assessments, and more face time communications with users in the organization about what they do and what users in similar organizations do.

Shifting Recruiting to Good Communicators and Business Savvy Individuals

With this change from technologists to analysts, the recruiting process in I.T. will shift from those who are good building, configuring, and managing servers and systems, to those who have exceptional communications skills, have business acumen, and are good business analysts. I.T. organizations will find they will think more like economists, looking to optimize marginal costs as opposed to technologists looking to build highly redundant and high performing systems. But this is the shift as services hosted in the cloud and paid for by consumption are best optimized and controlled rather than merely allowing users to consume an unlimited amount of capacity at an incremental cost to an organization.

From a costing model where some Web Conferencing service providers charge "per hosted conference session," other providers charge a flat monthly rate. Most organizations have just paid the "per conference rate" just like they have for years blindly paid for mobile phone charges. However when an organization is truly managing its costs of I.T., having a cost analyst track the cost of web conference calls versus the conversion to a flat fee service, the simple choice of selecting an appropriate vendor and their service plan can improve the bottom line for a business by $20,000/yr and in examples we've seen upwards of $500,000/yr.

The best run I.T. organizations are those that have tight controls over expenditures, not necessarily just cutting costs and pinching pennies, but truly analyzing usage and contracted rates. By looking for other competitive offerings from other providers and shutting down redundant servers at night and on weekends, an organization can better optimize their expenditures on I.T. services. This is no different than organizations shutting off lights at night and turning off air conditioning and heating systems during off hours as there's no reason to keep an empty office brightly lit and perfectly temperature controlled when nobody is in the office.

The make-up of the I.T. department is one where these more business savvy individuals will keep an eye on business operations and help the organization be more effective end-to-end at what it does.

Supporting Existing Technologist Roles

As a final comment on the changing role of I.T. personnel, not all I.T. Professionals will be replaced by a college educated Economics majors and English Literature majors, there's still a HUGE need for technologists in the technology industry. But the writing is on the wall that in today's I.T. environment, instead of nearly 100% technologists, I.T. organization are already finding a need for a blend of 20% business analysts and 80% technologists. And within 3-years, that model will be 40-60% business analysts, business savvy communicators, and managers compared to technologists. Still plenty of room for those with deep down valuable technical skills, however when half the jobs going to non-technology specific individual, it begs the need for either skill re-training or drastic shifts in the personnel that will make up the I.T. department in the near future.

It's these changes in the make-up of I.T. that have begun as organizations shift their I.T. services to hosted cloud environments. Additionally, as a more tech savvy workforce, requiring less handholding, become the norm in the business environment, the distribution of technical knowledge throughout an organization will change the focus of what I.T. will do day in and day out, I.T. has changed and will further change over the next 5-10 years, and as the changes will occur, organizations will adapt to the changing environment.

Part IV:
The Future of I.T. as a Business Enabler

11 FOCUSING ON THE BUSINESS, NOT ON SERVERS

As organizations reassess and realign I.T.'s role in the new world of I.T., the shift of I.T. goes from being datacenter, server, and systems focused to being focused leveraging technologies to help improve business services. It's the final change from no longer being focused on blinking lights and late night problem solving, to being proactive on things that I.T. never seemed to have the time to get around to in the past.

I.T.'s future isn't necessarily jumping right into directly improving frontline point of sales systems, inventory management systems, or production systems analysis and optimization. There is still another step that I.T. can help organizations focus on, and that's in the area of improving security, communications, and resource management.

Helping the Enterprise be More Proactive on Security Threats

For the past half-decade, cybersecurity has been front page news. A week doesn't go by without some story of some large enterprise hacked or compromised, with private information, financial information, or organization documents accessed and exposed. When I.T. was struggling to simply keep systems operational 24x7x365, finding time in a day to be proactive on security just was difficult to accomplish. However with daily operational tasks being handled by cloud services providers, and automation tools and solutions offloading many mundane tasks off of I.T., I.T. organizations have now found the time to be proactive with security.

Addressing Data Leakage Protection

A shift over the past few years has been transitioning from a focus of firewall protection of an organization's "edge" to that of data leakage protection. The reason for the shift is that edge protection assumes the organization can clearly define where the edge of its network is. In the cloud and mobile world, the edge now basically includes everything, from enterprise datacenter assets to cloud hosted environments to every single mobile phone, tablet, and laptop used by enterprise employees virtually anywhere at any time.

Data leakage protection instead focuses on the data, not on the edge. When data is properly categorized, the data can be prevented from "leaving" trusted organizational systems. Instead of trying to prevent external intrusion to some undefined edge, the focus is providing solid protections on key pieces of information that should never leave the organization's control.

The three components to create a functional data leakage protection system is to identify authorized individuals that should have access to information, classification of the data who should have access to the data, and policy-based controls that determines what information under what type of classifications should be available and accessed by certain individuals. By default, no one should have access to any classified assets, and by privilege rights, access is granted to approved individuals. Additional details on the three components are covered in subsequent sections of this chapter.

Leveraging Identity as a Service

Identity is a key component of the data leakage protection triangle. One of the core services that typically remains in the on-premise datacenter toward the very end of the modernization is the organization's identity system. Most organizations rely on Microsoft's Active Directory as the basis for user identity. Almost inevitably, the Active Directory has connectors that link Active Directory on-premise to cloud services like Office 365, Salesforce.com, Microsoft Azure, and the like. The end solution for identity typically takes one of two forms.

One solution for enterprises is to retain Active Directory on-premise as a key authentication point for users in each site. Active Directory has already been consolidated from a distributed site model to a centralized datacenter model as servers and applications have undergone consolidation to corporate datacenters. In other cases, as applications have distributed out to various cloud points, and datacenters being shutdown, we've seen Active Directory being distributed back down to organization site level.

Another solution for enterprises with respect to identity is to move the identity source to a cloud hosted model. Microsoft Azure Active Directory is a cloud-based centralized identity solution integral to Office 365 email authentication that many enterprises now have in place. As users logon to their email and authenticate to Azure Active Directory from their laptops, mobile phones, and tablets, the users just need a cloud-based authentication point like Azure AD and do not have a need for an on-premise Active Directory.

Azure Active Directory also provides multi-factor authentication that extends logon and password authentication to include another validation mode that might include a phone text message challenge, phone call challenge, or an email verification for access. This integrated security extends the basic functionality of Azure Active Directory into a more secure authentication model.

The basic Azure Active Directory in Office 365 can be extended to a Premium subscription that adds the capability of single sign-on of user logons to access 3000+ external applications like Salesforce.com, Box.com, American Express Travel, ADP, Workday, Google, and the like. Having a single authentication mechanism extended to ALL enterprise applications helps the organization gain control of user access to applications, and eliminates users from having to remember multiple logons and passwords. And when an employee is terminated, their access to ALL enterprise applications can be immediately terminated without I.T.'s need to go into dozens of applications and manually remove an individual's access to multiple applications.

And recent updates to Azure Active Directory include Domain Services that enable Azure ADDS to have servers and systems "join" the cloud-based directory and provide policy enforcement without the need for traditional on-premise domain controllers. This cloud-based directory with integrated multi-factor authentication, single sign-on to 3rd party apps, and policy-based enforcement provides organizations a complete solution without the need to deploy, manage, and distribute authentication servers throughout the enterprise.

Leveraging Automated Threat Protection

After an organization gains control of user logon and access to information, an extension to this functionality is to ensure attempts to compromise the organization's security is identified and thwarted. Automated threat protection monitors for brute force attacks on user logons, alerts the organization when a user's credentials are simultaneously used in two different parts of the world, and common attacks are proactively thwarted, minimizing the threat to the security of the organization.

Implementing Content Classification and Policy-based Controls

Completing the security triangle for data leakage protection is the ability for the organization to properly classify content, and apply policies that allow for access of key content by specified individuals. Organizations should not manage all data the same, otherwise it spends a lot of time and resources managing 80% or more of its data that has little or no business asset value. By classifying content, the organization can pick the 5%, 10%, 20% of the data it deems most sensitive, and then the organization can allocate more resources to protect that data.

The creation of policies on what data should be accessed by which users ties the final pieces together for the organization. It is these policies that an I.T. department, typically in conjunction with internal and external legal counsel can define, identify, manage, and protect content of the enterprise. This data leakage protection process is something that most I.T. departments haven't had the time to get around to in the past, that can keep the I.T. department busy for some time working through all of the processes necessary to help the organization digitally protect itself.

Improving Organizational Collaboration and Communications

Another core area that I.T. departments have jumped in to post application and datacenter modernization has been in improving organization collaboration and communications. For many organizations, collaboration has been simply utilizing the same tools that the organization has been using for years, or a relatively new tool that a handful of users jump on to use, but not a lot of organizational thinking went in to the tool on its applicability to meet the communications needs of the enterprise.

An assessment of what users internal and external to the organization do in terms of communications, along with an assessment on best practices on how other organizations leverage the latest technologies in their communications and collaboration can help an enterprise consider and select a solution that may be more appropriate for the organization as a whole.

Modernizing Voice and Video Communications

Along with an assessment on the collaboration and general communications tools that could be selected by the organization for more suitable fit to the needs of the enterprise includes the review of modernized voice and video technologies. Most organizations have phone systems and voicemail systems implemented, although in this day and age of emails, instant messaging, and mobile phones, the actual usage of traditional "phone systems" really needs to be evaluated.

For many organizations, modernization of telephony has included the elimination of old style PBX and even Voice-over-IP telephony systems where every employee has a phone number and voicemail box. When surveyed, an organization may find fewer than 5% or 10% of the users in the organization can even remember the last time they got a phone call or voicemail through the company phone system. As much as it is "nice" to have a centralized phone system, the cost of phones, telephony equipment, phone lines, and phone trucks typically starts off at thousands of dollars and quickly escalates to millions of dollars a year that organizations spend. An assessment whether everyone needs a corporate phone number and in many cases the elimination of the enterprise phone system for a large group of users can save an organization a lot of money every year.

Additionally, the use of integrated person to person voice and video conferencing solutions like Microsoft Skype or Google Hangouts that are part of integrated suites can be a good replacement for an organization, and fulfill all inner office and site to site communications for those who no longer need direct phone lines.

Improving on the Management of Diverse Endpoint Systems

Another big area in the post datacenter and application modernization roadmap is gaining control over all endpoint devices in the enterprise. Since backend applications are for the most part hosted and out of the control of I.T., being able to control and manage endpoint becomes the focal point of security policy implementation and data leakage protection policy enforcement.

Most organizations have some type of patch management system in place, however most of the times the management system only takes care of Windows-based system. Or if the organization has some type of management system to address Apple Macs, it's a completely different system. And yet another completely different system to manage mobile phones and tablets.

With the dust settled in I.T. eliminating the need for a heavy hand in building, configuring, and managing servers, I.T. can now focus on selecting and implementing a holistic endpoint management solution for the enterprise. A single solution that can manage ALL endpoint devices, whether it is a Windows desktop or laptop, Apple Mac, iPhone or iPad, or Android device is important for a holistic management strategy.

Being able to set one policy and have it applied across all endpoints uniformly will help I.T. ensure that security policies are strongly enforced not just on some devices, but enforced on all devices in the enterprise.

Exploring Data Analytics and Predictive Learning Solutions that May Benefit the Enterprise

As I.T. organizations address and update management tools, security, and policy-based management solutions, there's a whole area around data analytics and predictive learning that have taken root in organizations helping leverage data and turn that information into solution focused benefits to the enterprise.

Many I.T. organizations have started dabbling in data analytics by capturing security logs, endpoint access logs, user application access logs, network traffic data, and security policy enforcement data to aggregate information to understand who is accessing what, from where, and when to create correlations on existing data. This dabbling also enables I.T. to better understand the data analytics tools, how to utilize new languages like R, and run predictive learning models on data.

With an understanding of the power of the analytics tools, there are so many things an I.T. organization can do to use the same tools in analyzing frontline data coming out of sales, manufacturing, development, operational logistics, and other line of business data sources in the enterprise. By helping the organization better achieve a return on investment, increase sales, increase inventory turnover, and minimize logistics response times, I.T. will be empowered to help their organization increase revenues, decrease costs, and/or better utilize resources.

It is these changes where the evolution of I.T. from being a cost center pushing around email messages, backing up files, and performing mundane system patching routines to being an enabler on the business frontline is the direction of I.T. in the new world that I.T. will play in.

12 ALIGNING BUSINESS NEEDS WITH I.T. FULFILLMENT

As I.T. begins to better understand the overall strategy of the organization, as well as it starts to better understand how individuals within the organization function to do their jobs day in and day out, I.T. can then align its technology initiatives to better fulfill the needs of the business.

Mapping Technologies Directly to Business Needs

I.T. has focused the tools of the business to basic functions like email, word processing, general Web access and line of business applications. However those are just the basic tools that users need and the challenge has been that I.T. has been listening to their vendors and seeing what their vendor bundle within the licensing agreement rather than listening to the employees of the company to better understand what the users truly need to get their jobs done.

The proliferation of cloud-based tools has actually helped I.T. better understand the needs of its user base by seeing what tools and solutions (like DropBox, Salesforce, Google docs, SkyDrive, etc.) departments are using. It's not that every department is using the exact same tool, but there are similarities between the tools in use. So while one department might be using Box.com to store files and another department in the organization is using DropBox and another department is using SkyDrive, effectively the users across the enterprise are using some form of file storage and file sharing solution. And likely, after interviewing users and seeing what they use the cloud storage for, I.T. typically finds users are looking for a repository that they can access content from any of their devices (PCs, Macs, iPads, Android phones, etc.) and from anywhere (office, home, while traveling, etc.). Additionally, they can selectively share content with others outside of the organization. This basic universal file storage and sharing functionality has not been easy with traditional corporate enterprise tools. Traditional file systems were not accessible from outside the organization unless the user VPN'd into the network. Most corporate file systems did not provide the ability to share content with users outside of the organization and many corporate file sharing solutions might work great with a Windows-based PC, but had limited support for Macs, iPads, and mobile phones. So by understanding what users are using and doing, the technology that I.T. needs to identify and embrace in its I.T. services has to fulfill on these types of requirements demanded by its user base.

Sorting Needs to the Importance in Business Success

Just like with any list of needs, the key is to sort the needs and prioritize them so that I.T. can focus on the most important business solutions first. Of course the huge concern for I.T. organizations right now is the fact that there are a lot of these external cloud-based services where sensitive business documents are stored, without any security oversight, so the organization wants to move quickly to lock down content and protect information as quickly as possible. However rather than blocking access and preventing access to external information, the organization can sort business user needs into importance around business success, and then I.T. can get its arms around the technology solution needs in proper order.

Sorting Needs to the Fundamentals of Business Operations

The fundamentals of business operation are typically help the organization meet its business goals. In many organizations, it's the things that help increase revenues that contribute directly to business profitability.

When properly implemented and supported, those tools can hopefully help contribute to the success of the organization. From a technology standpoint, it might be tools that help sales individuals better target customer needs, which might be a client relationship management tool, or data analysis tools that crunches and processes data. Or it could be public awareness tools that help individuals within an organization better communicate with the organization's customers, that are of most benefit to the organization.

For many organizations, e-mail is a fundamental business tool, as users may use email to communicate with customers. Others may find transaction processing tools like ERP tools as mission critical for the business in terms of accepting and processing orders for shipment. Every organization has fundamental business needs that are supported by technology, and those tools that have the most impact on the success of the business are the ones that are typically prioritized for fulfillment in I.T.'s strategy implementation roadmap.

Reconciling Needs and Establishing I.T. Priorities

Reconciling needs may sound very similar to sorting fundamental business needs and priorities, but the focus here is I.T. priorities. There may be conflicting priorities that need to be addressed, and those may need to be rolled up to management to prioritize what is deemed most important to the organization. One example is an outward facing client solution that may drive sales up, however at the same time a security concern like customer and confidential legal information stored unprotected in external cloud storage services may need to be addressed promptly as well. Effectively one priority can improve business revenues, whereas another priority addresses data leakage due to lack of security controls.

In cases where there are conflicting business priorities, a business decision needs to be made to determine what the organization will prioritize. Many times, leveraging contract resources can allow an organization to do two or more things at the same time. Alternatively, the organization can do a risk assessment and while protecting confidential information is extremely important, if the data has been hosted externally at a cloud provider for the past 2 years, then what's another few more weeks to get around to tightening down the security on the external content. There are pros and cons, and establishing I.T. priorities can address the timing and fulfillment of execution on I.T. initiatives within the enterprise.

I.T.'s Success is Measured on Business Success

What we've seen over the past couple years is a shift in the measurement of whether I.T. is successful or not. In the past, I.T. measured its success typically by its attainment of some measurement of service level reliability of I.T. systems. If the organization's goal is 99.99% uptime, then the organization drives to that measurement and says it is successful because systems were always operational.

However, the more recent measurements of I.T. success have been based on the success of the business. When I.T. can associate increases in profitability with the introduction of a key sales tool or data analysis tool that helped the organization be more effective selling, then I.T. can show measurable contribution to the success of the organization. Or I.T. can directly translate the lowering of costs in the organization, like the decrease in long distance phone call bills, or the reduction in travel costs through the introduction of Web Conferencing or Web-based telephony solutions. The Web-based solution can better support users to communicate over existing data connections rather than using phone line services that charge per minute.

When the organization has the opportunity to grow and expand and to do so without direct linear increases in costs, this becomes a win for the I.T. department, if its services were key to that measurement of success within the business.

Focusing on Business Results, not Operational Capacity

Lastly, another metric for measurement is the shift from measuring I.T.'s value in terms of meeting operational capacity - shifting to measuring I.T.'s ability to directly address business results. If employees of an organization can communicate effectively with their clients using fewer travel days going to go and meet clients in person: not only are there direct savings in travel costs, but the employee can be spending the time normally consumed by travel to be communicating with other clients and helping expand the business.

The shift to cloud-based services with elastic capacity eliminates the need for the I.T. department to track and manage operational capacity. Instead, I.T. can now focus its time and effort on adding additional services, providing better methods of communications, and directly focusing the efforts of the business to grow and expand its services to the community.

ABOUT THE AUTHOR

Rand Morimoto, Ph.D., MBA, CISSP, MCITP: Dr Morimoto has a unique blend of deep technical knowledge and expertise, and an academic background in organizational behavior and organizational management. Dr Morimoto describes himself as a "tinkerer" of technologies, rolling up his sleeves and beta testing technologies months and years before the products are released to the general public. And not just one brand or solution of technologies, but his insight to what organizations want, what works, and what should be developed leads Dr Morimoto to being invited to participate in the early adopter programs of most of the key products and service providers in the industry.

Dr Morimoto is a deep-rooted academic, a lover of knowledge and information that led him to pursue his studies in an MBA program, a Doctoral program, and ultimately in the role of being on the governing board of a well-known academic institution.

Dr Morimoto blends the theory of economics and his expertise in organizational behavior and organizational management with his knowledge of the tech industry, resulting in the content highlighted in this book.